Death Poems

Poetry by Albert de Lorenzo

OddBrain Press

Leicester, North Carolina

Also by Albert de Lorenzo

Taken Aback in Passing 2009
Of Aging Angst 2011

Published by
OddBrain Press
PO Box 2045
Leicester, NC 28748

Death Poems
Poetry by Albert de Lorenzo
Cover Design by Albert de Lorenzo

ISBN 978-0-9762258-2-9

Dedicated to
Sharon Anne McCollum
Herta Johanna De Lorenzo

Verlin Manus
Mildred Manus
Jesse Manus
Chris Buckner
Paul R. Hughes, Jr.
Julescom
Marz Kelly

Contents   Page

by Don Hughes and Albert de Lorenzo

Yearning Eternity

Yearning Eternity
I reach forth
with spreading wing,
from my death-bed birth.

Left Yearning am I.

Fearing Eternity
I reach forth
with broken wing,
from my death-bed curse.

Passed through with a sigh

Death Dawns on Me

Tee Hee, Tee Hee,
cartoon eyes turn to (X)(X)s,
soon they are back
doing it again, doing it again.

Boo Hoo, Boo Hoo,
see Scruffy lay still,
it's funny HA HA funny,
no (X)(X)s in his eyes.

Occasionally people die.
I don't notice them, don't notice them,
though occasionally
I recognize Death's name.

They start dropping like flies
all around me, like flies,
yet they always belong
to someone else.

Death does not touch me,
does not touch me,
then without warning,
I recognize all its names,

Names Death drapes around it's shoulders.
Funny,
who was that behind my eyes just now?
Tee Hee, Tee Hee.

Holy Thursday

Parochial school incarceration
as a young boy you see,
forced to march in my uniform
next to some kid I hated.

Face scrubbed clean by a sadistic nun,
stomach lurching from the castor oil
the church uses to subdue unruly children,
marching still, innocent face miserable.

Black hooded nuns with their rulers
ready to crack already sore knuckles,
slapped in the back of the head so often
I named them Sister Larry, Sister Curly, Sister Moe.

Herded through the Gates to Hell,
kneeling in front of wooden pews,
our little red faces raised in fear and wonder
at the violence of death hanging over the altar.

What a God,
what a Father,
murdered His only son,
what would he do to us?

Grandfather's Poem

My mother, shocked by my words,
speaks to her long dead father,
apologizing for my poetry.

Did he roll over in the grave,
his eternal sleep disturbed,
by my words, or hers?

Did he open his long dead eyes,
squinting into the darkness,
and turn his good ear to us?

Did he speak in return,
his words echoing
down the corridor of time?

Mother, what did he say,
tell me please,
did he like my poem?

Nine Lives

Five-year old boys are indestructible.
I believed this as I was swept overboard,
drowning in the Atlantic Ocean
halfway between Italy and America.

I was murdered when I was eight.
An army officer strangled me,
spurting semen in my ass when
someone knocked at the door.

In Reform School,
at the age of twelve,
I was beaten to death
by a black boy my age.

When I was fifteen,
a Puerto Rican drug dealer
slit my throat with a switchblade
for spilling the cocaine.

I almost made eighteen
but six cowboys
jumped out of a pick-up truck
and kicked me to death.

A week after my twenty-first,
a pickpocket crushed my skull
with a brick, when I told him
to get out of my workplace.

At the age of thirty-six
I died a slow painful death
my lungs rotted away from
smoking four packs a day.

When I was forty-two,
my children and I were shot
to death by an angry man
as we walked in the desert.

I finally died of old age
at one hundred twenty-five,
greeting Death
as a familiar friend.

Child God

He is a cruel unjust god,
tearing them limb from limb
without the slightest thought,
killing them by the thousands,

pitting them against each other
in vicious fights to the death,
murdering entire communities
for the sheer pleasure of it.

Adult or child makes no difference,
all are fair game to this monster.
Some he crushes to death,
others writhe in the agony of fire.

Fortunately, he soon loses interest,
moving on to other pursuits,
leaving the insects of the world
to live their lives in peace.

Old Jimbo

I swing my arm in a circle
over and over again,
then with a sickening feeling,
the chicken body flies high overhead.

Thudding to the dusty earth,
blood pooling muddy,
flies at the ready,
I don't like it.

Old Jimbo walks over,
picks the chicken up,
"good job boy," he says,
"good job."

It Was So Cute

I found it crawling by the pond.
It wasn't much bigger than
an earthworm.

I carried it to the house,
turning my hand all the way,
as it curled around my fingers.

I was so excited,
I could barely wait
to show my Dad.

He came through the screen door,
told me to put it on the floor,
and stomped it.

"Copperhead," he said.

Puppy Love

You whimper as I approach,
squirming joyfully through the pain,
and lick your tears from my hand.

I stroke your head one last time,
put the gun to the back of your skull,
and pull the trigger once.

Your pain filled eyes look
confused, as the bullet rattles
around your brainpan.

Then you sigh one last time,
eyes brief with love,
finally, at peace.

In This Heated House

It is frosty out there,
only crows
and clear sky.
Sun yet
under covers,
reluctant to get up.

It is stone cold,
bone cold,
all alone cold,
even in this
heated house
I shiver inside.

A shirt from the dryer
helps momentarily,
a cup of hot coffee too,
but Death's nearness
keeps me from
the warmth of joy.

It is frosty out there,
only crows
and clear sky.
Sun yet
under covers
reluctant to give up.

Scarecrow's Lament

The gangs of crows
are gone from this valley,
leaving an uneasy silence
in the wake of their absence.

A lifelong pair or two
picnic on road kill
by the side of the road,
nearby trees empty of lookouts.

Bird Flu stalks the land
on tiny insect wings,
bringing doom to majestic birds
from coast to coast.

Wind rustles through dry cornfields,
earworms now the only threat,
munching away to the sad songs
of a nation of lonely scarecrows.

Trimmed to Pieces

I was just hanging out,
twisting in the breeze
until I lost my grip
and twirled to ground.

I lay in the shade
missing the hot sun,
wondering what
would become of me.

It wasn't long before
the leaf cutters came,
trimmed me to pieces,
took me underground.

China Buffet

They never sound right
real gunshots,
three of them
make me look.

You walk slowly
from the China Buffet
to the edge of the street,
gun hanging in your hand,

looking at me sadly
while you wait.
Soon the helicopter light
centers you.

Policemen with drawn guns
creep at you from two directions,
megaphones blaring,
our locked eyes blocking it all.

I am glad
you put the gun down,
there could have been
two dead this day.

The Landlady

Paying my rent one day,
the landlady is staring
at my crotch as usual,
then she reaches out.

"Shouldn't be doing this,"
she says.
"Old enough to be your mother,"
she says.

I left her on the floor,
dress pulled to her waist,
rolled hose bunched at her ankles,
a whispered "thank you" in my ear.

The next week
I went to pay again.
There was a new manager,
"died," he said, "cancer."

Birthday, Deathday

I don't want to die
in my sleep, like so many
people do.

Wake me, wake me, please
don't let me miss this
one moment.

I have waited all my life
for this
day.

Full of Life

Every time we saw one
we would stop,
and they would run
looking, looking, looking.

They would take great delight
in finding children
of long ago,
pointing them out to me.

Look Dad,
this one was nine,
eleven,
three.

Laughing as they ran,
joyful,
full of life
my children.

How they loved graveyards!

On a Winding Back Road

The future beckons
from a passing graveyard.
The past stares out
of a school bus window.
The present peeks
from a chain gang bus.
A brief moment
soon forgotten.

The Wee Hours

You used to call me in the wee hours,
telling me that Charlie was there.
I would listen to you all night,
or rush right over some days.

God, you were a mess.
One foot missing three toes,
causing you to shuffle
as you walked.

One arm ending
in two skin covered bones,
like giant chop sticks
to pick up life with.

Only two fingers
on the remaining hand.
You could still pick your nose,
one of life's little pleasures.

Your shaggy face
tattooed with dark blue dots
from the shrapnel
that blew out your eyes.

You used to call me in the wee hours
with Charlie in your good ear
talking softly,
about killing you.

*Charlie- Viet Cong

Wednesday Morning

The deepness of my eyes startle me.
I never really noticed them before today.
You can look in a mirror for a lifetime,
and not notice the person on the other side.

As I towel off, I feel the scar on my shoulder.
It takes me back, and I get lost there.
The tools for the job have been strapped on
before I return to the present.

In my sunglasses, I kiss my children goodbye.
My wife touches my hand.
Hearing the bus, I run for it; the driver waits.
Smiling a greeting I nod to those I know.

I go to the middle as I have for years.
Several Jews greet me.
The bus is always crowded.
I praise Allah and detonate.

No Blindfold Please

Life is like a firing squad
of blind marksmen.
Many shots will miss,
but enough will hit,
that you will die
in the end.

Serial Morning

A hard night's work
is deeply satisfying,
quivering from exertion
she sits back, listening.

Birdsong envelops
early forest, sky
melds black to blood,
she sighs.

Her favorite time of day,
murder lying before her
under the blazing Sun,
a morning sacrifice.

Nothing

Time's edge,
a disorienting,
confusing abyss.

Can't make it out,
is it before time
or after time?

I squat and peer,
one eye, then
the other, nothing.

Turn and listen,
one ear, then
the other, nothing.

My nose flares,
one nostril, then
the other, nothing.

I step over the edge,
one foot, then
the other....

Fear Not the Bandit

My shaking hands accompany
slithering thoughts
lost in a dim boyhood past.

I dream of being murdered
by Bandits in Tibet
while sleeping in my tent.

My brain shakes with thought quakes.
Eyes staring at my fat belly
fearing a fast fat TV ending.

Alone

Age no longer creeps up on me.
No, it is a constant companion,
a lifelong friend sorely neglected.

No afterlife balm to sooth away its edge,
No Gods wait at the end of the road,
no Demons either, except my own.

Like age, they too are lifelong friends.
I won't be alone after all,
at least for a little while.

Framed Ancestors

Curled like a
couch corner cat,

fetal eyes roving
over framed ancestors,

soon I will hang
among them.

Death Says Hello

Death peeks into my mind every day,
and has for as long as I can remember.
I will be walking along, minding my own
and BANG. Death says a queasy hello.

A sense of helplessness overwhelms me,
there is not a damn thing I can do about it.
Death's Hello echoes throughout my years,
Yet I am thankful for the reminders.

I am happy in the oddest places,
where others are depressed,
or question, is life worth living,
I never question. Death said Hello.

Why

When does one reach that moment
when living stops and waiting begins?
Is that when the anger sets in,
when futility infuses all?

What triggers the dead emotion
of waiting for the inevitable end?
What brings life to a screeching halt
long before the body is ready?

Where does that leave us,
if we are young with many years,
if we are old with little time,
where, what, when, why?

Why do so many live the lie,
mind closed to life,
eating, sleeping, waiting,
waiting, waiting, waiting to die.

Did, Died, Dead

The crotch rocket is parked where you left it,
your days of 140 miles per hour are over.
Did you hear about…, they would ask,
they didn't have to finish, I knew.

Your many friends are in a state of shock,
though a few of us were not surprised,
those that really knew you
were surprised it took you so long.

It was so like you to tell one,
well if that's the way you feel
I'll just, just, just…
and you did, died, dead.

Was the note to your mother enough
do you think, to make up for
the image of you in her mind,
swinging slowly like a pendulum?

For Eternity

God lifts the lid of the coffin,
sticks His finger in the bullet hole,
looks into your cold dead eyes,
"I knew you would do this."

There is no breath of life,
no breath of death, the heart
silent, the soul departed,
riding motorcycles in Hell.

Racing Eternity neck in neck,
brimstone rooster tails, reaching
Heaven, dying embers at God's feet,
Demons cheering the last turn.

It's a straight run to the Pearly Gates,
Eternal Life in the lead, Death
close behind, cold dead eyes
seeing the bullet coming.

Dead, Dead, Really Dead

The ink flows from the tip of my quill
like blood from razor cut veins,
spreading the news on electronic parchment
that my friend is dead, dead, really dead.

Like a town crier of old,
I stalk the dark alleyway
of the Internet, screaming
words at the speed of light.

Total strangers turn and stare,
as the news climbs microwaves
to the satellites above, broadcasting
my friend is dead, dead, really dead.

I Told Them, I Told Them All

They buried you today
and I wasn't there,
didn't need to be really,
to see your cold dead body
with its broken face.

I wonder, did time slow down
at the crucial moment?
Did you see the bullet coming,
agonizingly slow, creeping
till it splattered your brains?

I can too easily see you
lying twisted, the tub
like a vase, your body
like a vine leading to
your red blooming head.

One of those exotic plants
that bloom every 47 years,
they are so frighteningly
beautiful, that once seen
are never ever forgotten.

You stand next to me
shifting your ghostly gaze,
grinning sardonically,
I told them Albert,
I told them all.

Whisper Them to Me

Many friends are angry with you
for taking your own life, jealous
I guess, for knowing your own time.
Locked in your concrete vault,

safe at last, your knowledge
of the future is complete.
Your friends live on in fear
of what you now know so well.

We used to discuss life,
the Universe, and everything
each time we met. Thinking
we knew the answers.

I am not angry, though I am
sad that you chose to go.
I'll miss our one minute
philosophical discussions.

Your new world, deep black,
its icy grip unbreakable, unrelenting,
is now your one and only friend,
holding you close and eternal.

You know the answers at last,
to the questions we always asked
in passing, on life's road.
Whisper them to me.

I Miss You

Knowing you, you probably felt bad
having cheated Death so many times,
felt that you owed him, and this
was as good a time as any.

Everyone is trying to find a reason
to blame themselves for your going,
like anything they could have said
or done could bear such weight.

You are oblivious of course,
now as well as then. So many
thought they had connected.
You looked right through them.

Well my friend, I don't feel bad.
I knew you were going all along,
and I started missing you long ago.
I will miss you for some time yet.

No More

We were different,
used to speak
of everything.
No more.

Words unspoken
now silent,
yours silent,
mine silent.

In the garden of stones,
your chosen home,
I marvel at the many
friends you have.

Surrounding you,
far as the eye can see.
In your cold holes,
you, one of many.

Once all different,
now the same.
I marvel at
your silence.

Julescom

A woman that I do not know
died today, five days after
we never met, and yet
we were friends to the end.

I do not know where she lived,
even so, I have sat in her bright and
cheerful living room, discussing
God's will with our old friend Death.

Stood behind her, looking
over her bathroom shoulder,
at our reflections in the mirror,
hers, mine and Death's.

Sat by her feather bed, while
she struggled with sleep,
tossing, turning her way awake,
death waiting by her side.

Hovered in the corner
of a white porcelain room,
watching as poison is
pumped into her veins.

I stand over her grave
maybe a dozen, maybe
a thousand miles away,
Death quiet beside me.

Five Days in April

The Doctor told me
that I have cancer,
treatments tomorrow,
and no more writing.

Will you write for me?

I'm very tired,
and must keep this short.
Thank you for the
poetic justice.

Your poetry has such impact.

Thank you for moving me.
For making me fight.
I am angry now,
and that is a good thing.

I wish I could be like you,

I have been reduced to drivel,
lilts, timing, rhymes.
Please, this is not me.
My brain has turned to puree.

if I only had a chance to grow up.

These are my last words,
the hospice beckons.
I am forever in your debt.
Thank you for befriending me.

You wrote beautifully today.

Without Warning

Without warning Death knocks on the door.
Chicken Shit that he is, he sends the messenger boy,
underpays the nurse to call me with the good news.

What the fuck! I'm not ready for this,
fuck me, I love you guys that took the trip before me,
I miss you terribly, wasn't planning on coming so soon.

I want to break everything, I hate everybody,
God, Damn it all to Hell.
I'm scared of that dark hooded bastard, he won't stop
until the entire universe is dark and cold and lifeless.

Chemo, Radiation shit, shit, shit! I don't care, yes, I do.
I don't want that crap, yes, I do.
Six months of misery, waiting to die, sick as a dog.

It isn't worth it, yes, it is.
I hate this, no, I don't.
They say I won't be able to write, yes, I will.

This is a horrible place, but when I squint my mind,
I can see, twisting and contorting through my tumors
veins of poetic gold, mother lode of unwritten poems.

My lifeblood begins to spill upon the page.

Read it, read me

forever.....

Remember Me

I feel it beat Rhythmic,
I feel it beat Rhythmic,
I feel it beat Rhythmic.
I feel it beat,
I feel it beat,
I feel it beat.
I feel beat,
I feel beat,
I feel beat.
My heart feels beat.
My mind feels beat.

My heart is no longer soft.
My mind is no longer at ease.
My thoughts are not gentle.
I don't like it here.
I am alone.
I cling to live.
I cling to exist.
Embrace me.
Know me.
Make me happy.
Remember me.

I found myself not long ago.
I thought I was lost, lost
till I was nudged by,
by two strangers.
Nudged by two strangers,
nudged back into my shin,
my comfortable skin.
Tonight, I look into the mirror,
crow's feet, laugh lines, grey on top,
Uncomfortable skin,
Shroud of a skin.

Today the Doctor Said...

sterile white music
plays soft background
We're ready to...
We're ready to...
We're ready to...
start your treatment now

off the side of the road
twice
off the side of the road
twice
to get sick
off the side of the road

I see a face
there is a tear
still bloody
a single tear
screaming for help
I see a face

upstairs I wash that face
in the mirror upstairs
I wash that face
with a single tear
I wash that face
screaming for help

my feather bed envelopes me
as I close my eyes
as I close my eyes
my feather bed envelopes me
as I close my eyes
another face emerges

I keep hearing over and over
over and over I keep hearing
something, something, something,
has gone wrong
over and over, over and over,
I keep hearing, something's wrong

Whisper to Me

Death, my lifelong friend,
have you news of my son and husband?
Tell them please, that I shan't be long.
The doctor tells me I will be next.

"…to be honest with you…"
No, lie to me Doc.
"…to be honest with you…"
…it don't look good…"

Death my lifelong friend,
what did God say,
He had to tell you something,
whisper it in my ear.

"We can start your Chemo,
we can start your Radiation,
Tomorrow, Tomorrow, Tomorrow,"
less than six months of tomorrow.

Death my lifelong friend,
I can't believe it,
I won't believe it,
Damn, I do believe it.

Just like that,
exit stage left.
Six months,
you have got to be kidding!

Death my lifelong friend,
Maaaaaaaaannn, I am not
looking forward to this.
To die.........ummmmmmmmm.

Can't seem to grasp it,
can't stop crying,
can't stop being angry,
can't stop being scared.

Death my lifelong friend,
How am I going to get through this?
I'm alone.. I'm going to die alone.
What do I do?? Whisper to me.

Tormented

My friend's pen,
overcome by reality,
overcome by the here,
overcome by the now,
stains the page,

with lifelines of ink,
birthing strange worlds,
worlds of fear,
worlds of anger,
worlds of defiance,

blood-soaking paper fibers
with tormented thoughts of life
with tormented thoughts of death
with tormented thoughts,
tormented.

Her gentile mind and soul
writhes like a butterfly
on God's display board,
Death repositioning the pin
at the Lord's command.

It's Not Personal, It's Business

Julie, Julie, Julie
how could you do me so wrong,
what do you mean
I came with no warning.

I took your grandmother,
I took your Aunt Lenor,
I took Jackie
and your cousin Mark.

I took your son,
I took your husband,
all warnings, warnings
that I was coming for you.

You do me wrong to fight me so.
I have taken hundreds of millions
since God commanded me
to do His dirty work.

You are just one
on a never ending road.
Please don't fight me so,
it's not personal, its business

Death Drops By

"Nice place you got here," Death says,
"kind of cheerful, not at all
what it looked like last month,
all dark, drawn and full of spider webs."

I can't believe it, he just comes in,
plops down on the sofa
like he owns the place,
Death on the sofa, on my sofa!

"Your different too," Death continues,
"figured you would draw the blinds,
again, draw them again,
try to hide from me, again."

"Julia," I whisper, "don't leave, I need you,
I am counting on you to get me through.
I will not let this defeat me.
I am not afraid," I look at Death and smile.

"Sorry about your son,
sorry about your husband,
God just has those days,
then he sends me."

"I am strong, vibrant and alive.
I have my sight,
I am not deaf,
I am blessed."

Death stands up and nods,
walking to the door, he turns,
"Yes, you are blessed,
I am not to take you straight away!"

I Wish I Knew

Lurking within dream sequences,
shadow-creatures of the mind
shade each passing day
with barely remembered puzzles.

Emerging from the subconscious
a growing foreboding
of unknown proportions,
a cataclysmic impact,

cutting from deep within.
Wounded and in need of healing,
it creeps closer,
feeding off my unknowing.

My thoughts eat voraciously,
a glutton for my fear.
I wish I knew.
Death lights my cigarette.

Still Alive

I am alive at 10pm,
tired, exhausted,
but still alive.

The bathroom mirror,
has a new face,
haggard and drawn,

leather skin shrouding
eyes circled dark,
touched gently

by old hands,
broken skin hands
with aching bones.

Like an apparition
I float down the stairs,
resting on the sofa.

"Dime short,
day late," I whisper,
"Dime short, day late."

Why Lord

I have come to terms
these last days,
finalizing my life,
marked for death.

With cunning,
my diluted self
thinks, hopes, lies
that I will make it.

A whisper of a day,
one word whisper,
life ending whisper
"Hospice," whispered.

I leave with deep regret,
with great displeasure,
my home, my sanctuary,
to embrace my defeat.

I cannot bear to go.
I am tired, tired, tired.
I ask God's helping hand
for the last time.

Give me strength,
give me wisdom,
give me dignity,
to die in your Grace.

Forgive me,
I have no right,
for hating You
for so long.

Forgive me
for not forgiving You.
Let me understand God,
why You take my life.

My inspiration,
my very breath,
not when I was ready,
but now when I am not.

You took by childhood,
standing silent, omnipresent,
watching the beatings, the
never ending sexual abuse.

I had nowhere to go,
nowhere to turn,
no one to hear my cry,
not even You.

You gave me a loving man,
then blessed us with a son.
I knew how big a heart could be
a son, gone in a blink of an eye.

Our hearts of pain and misery,
asked, "Why Lord?"
Then in a blink of an eye,
the man of my dreams.

You stand silent,
omnipresent,
sending Death to collect me
in the blink of Your eye.

I have nowhere to turn,
no one to hear my cry,
when You close my eyes
will my tears finally stop?

The Beat of Each Heartbreak

Alone again, fighting my way
Through levels of DOOM 3,
my wife fighting her way, to
Death's house to see her father.

She drives tired, in great pain,
physical pain, emotional pain
coursing through her veins
with the beat of each heart break.

I, her knight in tarnished armor,
Blast Death's demons, zombies,
killing waves of never ending fiends,
keeping Death occupied, distracted.

Under cover of my relentless attack,
my wife slips by Death and his minions,
crossing a million miles of danger
encircling her dying father with love.

A never-ending battle, to protect
loved ones from our shared fate.
We wage it daily, yearly, for life,
Never giving in until the end.

Death is my Houseguest

Death is a guest in my home,
everywhere I turn, everything
I touch, everything, everything
reminds me, Death is near.

Came by caravan late one night,
wheeled, walked his charges in
on a fresh built wheel chair ramp,
dumping the dying into our lives.

Strangers came the next day,
delivering a Death Bed,
Death Industry workers galore,
like evil moths to a flame.

Midnight frights send us scurrying
across a rain soaked cityscape,
carrying our desperation and fear,
wrapped in this husk of a human.

So many rely on an extended dying,
for their lively-hoods, their denial,
playing yo-yo with Death,
hiding their fear behind other's misery.

The Death Bed

The Death Bed came today,
in such an ordinary manner,
delivered by truck, unloaded
on the clock, under gray skies.

Put together by a stranger,
most soft spoken and polite,
the air mattress left filling,
hand controls all tested.

How does he feel, delivering
highways to hell,
stairways to heaven,
Death Beds, one size fits all.

He is gone now to his
young life, with no end
in sight, leaving us
to face our mortality alone.

Dutiful Daughter

Like a saint of old, my wife kneels,
washing the pus and blood from
her father's diabetic legs, bloody
stumps that barely hold up his
cancerous body, she barely holds up.

She plays hide and seek with the piles
of worthless garbage that mother's
senility insist are family heirlooms,
great treasures gathered over a life,
a lifetime spent hoarding junk mail.

Her brother, once a reluctant care giver
lies dying alone in his bed, racing
his father to the finish line of life,
no longer sullen, hateful, as before
his terrible understanding of truth.

We speak words of comfort daily,
building a verbal life raft of love,
clinging to it as the sea of life,
the sea of death, rages around us,
our love will prevail even this.

The day will come, all too soon,
with two more men laid to rest,
a forgetful widow, confused,
wondering when hers will come,
following her daughter home.

Our Own Fear

The ambulance drivers take their time,
Death lays in the back almost sleeping,
they all know his time has come, too soon,
so why is he still here, still breathing?

His loving sister tries to protect him
from the indifference of the living
from caregivers who have stopped giving,
having long ago forgotten how to care.

He rests now uneasy, amongst strangers,
staring at the darkening ceiling, listening
to their inane banter of makeup and grooming,
silly laughter echoing from room to room.

How many others, behind thin walls,
project their dying fears, like him,
alone, a reminder of things to come
to those hiding behind medical degrees.

There is nothing more we can do,
they whine, nothing more, not even
look into his haunted eyes, lay a hand
on his tissue paper skin to comfort.

It is best to close his door, keep the air
flowing out of his room, wear masks
to protect him, or hide behind, avoid
his gaze, lest we see our own fear.

Dr. Death

The sudden awakenings,
midnight rides to hospital
Death backseat driving,
lonely red lights ignored.

Driving in a thick fog
both mental and real,
windshield opaque,
Demons wisp by.

The world sleeps fitfully
as we roll along, tires
spraying mist behind,
leaving a trail of tears.

An empty waiting room
beckons, sleepy attendants,
like roosting vultures,
stir at our approach.

Come in, Come in
they croak in unison,
lay him on this slab,
Dr. Death is on the way.

Dying Eyes

Dying eyes, like newborn eyes
seeing life for the first time,
shine with fearsome knowledge,
radiating truths too terrible.

Ghosting through final days,
a creature of pure thought,
self-sorrow, false hope,
fought off resignation.

The betrayal of the body,
an awesome burden to bear,
yet the mind's desperation
far outweighs physical pain.

Spinning in the vortex,
existence drains away
at the speed of light,
at a snail's pace.

Pleadings for relief, release,
fall on a deaf God's ears,
echoing the end of time,
the silence of oblivion.

Bids Me Be Still

Your skeleton emerges slowly,
month by month,
week by week,
day by day,
hour by hour
minute by minute,
second by second,
breath by breath,
heartbeat by heartbeat,
tremor by tremor.

Your dying eyes peer inward
like two black holes
searching for the event horizon Soul
from which Life itself cannot escape,
Death itself cannot escape,
Eternity cannot escape.

A vulture on a limb of the Tree of Life,
I sit, hover if you will
above your death bed.
I wait to pick your carcass clean,
while you sleep, writhe in agony,
frown at life parading by your door,

a loud annoying life
you don't notice till I preen,
pluck your dying thoughts with my beak.
You open your eyes.

Death's demon is wearing your face,
staring through closed lids,
bids me be still.

These Dying Lives

Death comes bearing gifts,
mummified hands and
huge dying eyes.
Newborn eyes, seeing
life for the first time.

Parchment skin fingers
gracefully folding time,
accepting this final wisdom,
cupping a shifting eternity,
sifting the dust of oblivion.

Huge shining eyes,
brimming with clarity
belie shrunken heads
with wispy, silky hair,
spearing all they see.

What do they see,
these eyes, what do they
feel, these opaque hands,
what do they know,
these dying lives?

Sometimes a Lingering

It's hard to hide from Death,
She will find you out, tag
your dead, no matter where
or when you try to hide.

If She isn't ready for you,
someone close will begin
the drop, eternal free fall,
blessed oblivion at last.

It matters not to Her one bit,
a dying father, a brother
caregiver notwithstanding,
an Aunt recently out of mind.

She swirls on through, tag
your dead, tag your dead,
tag, sometimes a lingering,
She is so very busy after all.

He Sleeps

He lies twisted, contorted,
a gargoyle dream twitching
his life away, while visions
play out in REM sleep.

Fused eyelids sink inwards,
like strange skin pupils
staring into this world, from
a time and place far away.

Squirming open at last,
black obsidian glints
between mucus lashes,
retreating behind skin again.

He sleeps, this creature,
half Human, half Soul,
waiting for the moment,
the moment to say goodbye.

Each Touch

Your face, like chiseled stone,
aging a decade each month,
sixty years of character,
six months in the making.

Your hands encased
in shrink wrapped skin,
skeletal fingers, blue veined,
trace a road map to the end.

Thin legs with creased shinbones,
like freshly ironed dress pants,
lead to long delicate feet,
toes arching into the future.

Death sits by you
caressing your torment lovingly,
each touch a wasting,
each touch, a tremor of dark delight.

A sudden halt of breath,
a sudden halt of heart,
 an attentive lover Death,
each touch a long pause.

In the End

In the end, it is the eyes,
no longer focused on life,
shiny pupils peering into
the depths of heaven.

Like twin telescopes
staring fixed, floating
on the outer edge, riding,
cresting each dying breath.

The body gasping at
the speed of life's ending,
the eyes wide open,
greeting the unknown.

In the end, it is the eyes,
zooming into eternity
body crashing to earth
eyes like cracked ice.

Oblivion Express

Death departs without a word,
a final breath, more a sigh,
the thin ice of life giving way,
cracking his far away eyes.

His jaws motion once, twice,
swallowing the last of his pride,
the brain living out its eternity
in this fifteen minutes of refrain.

I sit with the body, others gone
paper-working the business of death,
his brain knows I am there, odd,
it gives me comfort to be with him.

My heart beats away the minutes,
beats away his eternity, beats away
faster and faster, matching soon
the wheels of the Oblivion Express.

Finger Pain

These fingers moments ago
caressing the forehead of death,
now curl around a cold drink,
stuff a last morsel into my maw,
write these very lame words.

How can they so quickly
move from the sublime
to the minutia of life,
brushing back unkempt hair,
picking an overly dry nose.

The mind is taken aback,
looks at them strangely,
blinks its eyes rapidly,
fanning back tears of pain,
they reach and wipe them away.

An Island in Time

It's been a long road,
full of dead ends,
spiraling cul-de-sacs,
straight horizon runs.

Either bare feet
or too tight shoes
on painful rocks,
or slicing glass.

Crowded with billions
all jostling for position,
jangled, mangled bodies,
road kill with each step.

Passing centuries only add to
the road of life, overflowing
like a raging river, crushing
over the cliff of oblivion.

Each an island in time,
swept ever faster,
Souls like lemmings
leaping into the unknown.

The Green Dot

You never did speak again,
at least you never answered
my pleas, never answered
my waves, never answered.

But the green dot
glowing by your name, two
sometimes three times a day
let me know you were there.

I thought the passage of time
would heal our wounds,
that the day would come
when you would wave back.

You were there day and night,
keeping the same odd and end
hours, it was just a matter of
time, and you would say Hello.

The green dot gave me hope
that we could set the past aside,
look towards the future only,
speak our hopes and dreams.

But you died in your sleep,
the green dot black and silent,
our odd and end clock awry.
We will never speak again.

Over the Shoulders of Strangers

My long dead son died today,
a quarter century after I buried
him in my heart, rotting there
till the day he died in his sleep.

The alarm was given, by a friend
of his, unknown to me, a town
crier heard half way round the world,
pulling the rusty blade from me.

I sent my grief on wings of prose,
shot from the sky by arrows of hatred,
mother snake and her daughters,
denying me entrance to the crypt.

From afar, as for so long, I look
over the shoulders of strangers,
gleaning every kernel of my son's
passing, gathering his leavings close.

A New Day

You died in your sleep they said,
but did you really,
or did you wake at that instant
and realize that it was the end?

Did your life flash before you,
your 36 years compressed into
a split second of eternity, before
sinking below waves of oblivion?

Were your last thoughts sad
over losing your past,
fearful of an unknown future,
comforted by a myth of an afterlife?

Did you speak, a last gasp of farewell,
righting wrongs, setting records straight,
casting aspersions, bargaining for
just one last chance?

Or were you stoic, at ease,
accepting of your fate, quiet,
as the night surrounding you
brightened into a new day?

My Stone Heart

I stand over your grave,
a thousand miles away,
your name, your life dates
chiseled on my stone heart.

You loved graveyards, running
as a child, finding the children,
look Dad, this one was 3, 6, 2,
full of life, full of laughter.

Your life and laughter gone,
only silence remains,
but I am used to that, it was
your way with me.

Your friends have already gone,
only four days from your death,
the condolences finished,
their lives rapidly moving on.

But I will come every day,
every night, every moment
of my life, in remembrance
of you, waiting in silence.

I will stand over your grave,
a thousand years from now,
my name, my life dates
chiseled on my stone heart.

Broken Hearts

In the hour of your death,
Seven Thousand, Two Hundred people
followed in your footsteps,
walking down the corridor of time.

In the twenty-four hours after,
One Hundred Seventy-Two
Thousand, Eight Hundred people
stepped into Eternity.

In the twenty-five days since,
Four Million, Three Hundred
Twenty Thousand people
slipped into Oblivion.

So it goes, two die every second,
of every minute, of every hour, of
every day. I cannot help but wonder,
how many broken hearts that is.

Memories Only

The body aches and moves slowly,
a sense of weariness has set in,
youth but a memory of times past,
the future ever shorter day by day.

Death begins to visit in earnest,
not a stranger taking strangers
to their final rest, but more intimate,
touching friends, family, ever closer.

Gardens of stones abound
down every road, around every curve,
on every hilltop, in every valley,
depositories of the rotting dead.

Walking the well-manicured paths,
pushing through the overgrown
and forgotten, new stones sparkle,
moss grown tablets nameless.

For each the ache is gone,
weariness ceased, death forgotten,
the future ever longer day by day,
memories only for the living.

Last Rites

The prodigal son sits by his Mother's
death bed, hearing her confession,
laying on his hands, drawing guilt from
within her tormented soul.

He wrings it out like an old washer woman,
scrubs it out on the washboard of denial,
hangs it on her lifeline to dry in the breeze
of forgiveness, grants her the grace of ease.

This frail creature, the source of his own life
stands on the cliff of eternity, fearfully searching
the horizon of oblivion for a glimpse of home,
breathing as if in labor, birthing her own death.

Her eyes weary and sad, painfully joyful
smile with resignation, at the dawning of truth,
as her sins of omission are washed away
by the Extreme Unction lies of her son.

He leaves her at rest in her mind,
travels his years of anger and resentment
all the way home, swallowing bitterness,
spitting it out to fester on the roadside.

The Poems that Scare Her

My books of poetry are
hidden in mother's house.
She can't read them. She
won't read them anymore.

The words, sentences, ideas
of my poems scare her,
black ink on a white page
frighten her like a child.

She speaks to her dead father
apologizing for my poetry.
Reading them to him,
my one audience of the dead.

Does he sit on her lap, lay
his decaying head on her chest
as she rocks back and forth
reading my poems to him?

The poems that scare her,
poems she apologizes for.
And what does he think?
He is dead after all.

The Moss of Time

From beyond the final oppressive winter,
as the moss of time covers her crypt,
immortal words slant their way across
the shadow landscape of our modern world.

From a forest of eccentric seclusion,
distillations of mind escape the grasp of Death,
on odd and end pieces of paper, aged words
continue to echo from eternity.

Time Ebbs and Flows

Lost in revelries of a lifetime
seconds drag by as centuries,
minutes flow like passing years,
hours follow as endless days.

I can no longer remember
yesterday, what was said,
thoughts of an hour ago gone,
this poem slipping away.

Time ebbs and flows
in such strange ways,
short spans an eternity,
an eternity long gone.

The ink on this parchment
barely dry, evaporating still,
like my chiseled name
wearing away on this tomb.

Callous Poet

In the darkness, he strokes
my quivering brain until
it spurts neurotransmitters
across synaptic gaps,
cascading emotions.

Left limp with the aftereffect
of this cerebral climax
I sit back in reflection
of the poem just read,
examine mixed emotions
joy, embarrassment, anger.

How can this poet long dead,
reach out across Time,
have his way with me,
then so callously
toss me aside?

Whence We Came

Sitting at the end of the world
watching icebergs calve off glaciers,
like the years of my youth
splitting from the totality of my life.

Falling into the sea, they float,
dissolving into the waters,
like my existence melding away
into the ocean of oblivion.

For both the glacier and I
it is only a matter of time
before we become one,
returning whence we came.

Silence, Blessed Silence

A winter wind howls, shrieks
in one ear and out the other,
tear blurry eyes freeze shut,
mustache like a frozen forest.

Muscles hardening over
softening bones, bloodsicle lungs
last gasping, heart flubbing
its end, brain draining away.

Ice mountains split, cracking,
shattering thin eardrums into crystals,
bringing silence, blessed silence,
then darkness, blessed darkness.

Twenty thousand years pass before
the sun warms the glacier enough,
tourists are astonished, fascinated
by a hand sticking out of the ice.

Event Horizon

Infinite oblivion envelops
spasms of consciousness
lifting eye stalks above
the event horizon of Birth.

Infinite reality envelops
consciousness, spasming
bulging eye stalks of disbelief
at light's vibration of Life.

Infinite oblivion envelops
spasms of consciousness,
dim eyestalks swirling beyond
the event horizon of Death.

Echoes Off the Wall

Organic echoes whisper
off undulating placental walls,
filling freshly formed ears
with ghostly vibrations.

Echoing synapse to synapse
this whisper of Beginning.

Cacophonous echoes kaleidoscope
off curving brainpan walls,
creating carbon consciousness
with billions of neural transmissions.

Echoing human to human
this psychobabble of Living.

Black-body echoes at 3 degrees Kelvin
off walls of the infinite universe,
reflecting from microwave antennas
with Cosmic Background Radiation.

Echoing galaxy to galaxy
this Big Bang's Ending.

The Shore of Infinity

How does one turn the ship of life around,
trapped in currents of years gone by,
buffeted by screaming gales of reality,
narrowly missing hidden shoals below?

There are no charts to guide the way,
no instruments of position or drift,
often no crew but a lonely Captain
peering dejectedly into thickening fog.

Thousands of ports stretch into the past,
all missed opportunities to disembark,
sad memories of a life blindly misspent
following a foregone conclusion.

The sages with their wise advice
long ago abandoned ship, leaving
each Captain alone at tiller,
steaming circles on the endless sea.

Staring into misty wheelhouse windows
at old, tired, and dim reflections,
barely illuminated by a drowning sun
sinking below the distant horizon.

The enormity of this infinite ocean
yields not to the spinning wheel,
useless rudders fishtailing behind,
wallowing between two crests of life.

How does one turn the ship of life around
before the current of Time runs out,
leaving a rusting hulk, or broken timbers
strewn along the shore of Infinity?

This Ancient Holy Place

Through the cold mist of my breath
I see three empty arches,
once magnificent stained glass windows,
now filled with leafless vines and thorns.

It is stone cold, bone cold
under a sliver of moon.
Pinprick stars pierce
through a black sheen.

The altar top is broken
pieces scattered on the floor,
a creature of the night kneeling,
wailing at the stars above.

Shivering clear to my Soul,
I do not want to believe,
yet the hardness of this marble
insists to the reality of this place.

The sharpness of my slightest sound
raises my senses to a razor's edge,
brings the creature's mad gleam upon me,
his wails echoing throughout the ruins.

Soon the creature comes for me,
stars above begin to swim,
fangs sink into my throat,
the only warmth in this place.

How beautiful it is!
It seems so natural,
this ancient holy place,
my unexpected death.

Silence of the Crypt

The silence of the crypt is
broken by rat scurry echoes
all along the Great Hall.
Thousands emerge from
piles of castle rubble.

Dashing, stampeding
into the chapel, crushing
against the altar, raging,
a roiling river of rats
whirlpool into the crypt.

Silently surrounding
a dark sarcophagus,
they sit, eyes twinkling,
whiskers twitching,
sighing into the night.

Unspeakable Presence

Nothingness gives icy comfort,
sudden coldness astonishes,
dying life light illuminates,
forced silence surrounds.

My hushed breath brings
thoughts of my Lord,
frightened creatures scurry
at his unspeakable presence.

Christ's wounds razor me,
forehead, feet, hands, heart,
my lifeblood vaporizes.
An ancient Heart speaks Death.

Silently I worship this sullen God,
a trillion years of sadness to come,
no more refuge, no more altar rituals.
Nothingness gives icy comfort.

They Are Calling

It is getting late, I should be in bed
not nodding out over this parchment,
dipping quill into ink, scritching,
scratching my way into obscurity.

Many a candle has met its demise
long before the words ran out,
oftentimes fowl feather etchings
are all that attest to a night's work.

Ink bottle emptied by my futile efforts
to empty my head of its torments,
to drain my Soul of its Immortality,
staining Time itself with my epitaph.

Inhaling the acrid smoke of burning
wick and funeral pyres prompts
a greater effort, time is short,
I must write it all down, now.

The candle flame has met its death
as will we all, as will I, hear them
creaking, groaning wheels bearing
a great weight, coming ever closer.

They are calling me, I must go,
I am so tired, I feel so heavy.
They are calling me, calling me.
Bring out your dead.

Kneeling Before Barren Altars

Is the futility of hope,
in a hopeless universe cruel,
or is cruelty an artificial hue
applied with layers of denial?

Dust to dust, ashes to ashes.
In denial of our handful of dust,
of our forbidden knowledge,
in fear we choose to live.

We build unreal fortresses,
fearful, neither alive nor dead,
denying till the end,
our own undoing.

Death taps the shoulder,
at times lightly, and we lose someone.
Within us we plant the corpse
in a garden of stones and rubbish.

The truth takes these moments to sprout
deep within, and chills with sudden frost.
Oblivion raises its ugly head at last.
How can we deny now?

Lying in our satin cases, we are nothing.
Withered time leans out into the hushed room.
Think dead men, your time is coming.
Will you continue wasting your precious life in denial?

In an instant, life is over.
What ever shall we do?
Why are you wasting your life?
Why are you waiting for the knock upon the door?

Just like that, it is time.
The city of the dead awaits us,
gaining an unknowing population
each and every moment, each and every day.

Why will we not believe,
why do we hurry on our way?
Our last clutch at salvation sinks unheard.
Our last breath an unbelieving.

Even in the midst of acceptance,
denial creeps in throbbing,
oh how badly we need the indifference of the dead
toward death itself, if we are truly to live.

It is strange that so many yearn for death.
Spend their lives building an afterlife,
arriving at the end of the meal
without remembering a single bite?

This yearning for death I do not understand.
My dead hands with broken fingernails,
would claw their way back to life,
were there a way.

If only there were gods and devils,
deities to snatch us from the jaws of death,
swaddle us in their love, rock us
in the crib of eternity, hum us the ultimate lullaby.

How many are buried since time began?
How many more before time ends?
And if there is no beginning, no ending to time,
how many will we bury then?

From the moment of our births
we chant our lives away,
kneeling before barren altars,
the crypts below filled to bursting.

Unusual Charm

A sky so deep I can almost believe,
almost believe in the imminence
of Rapture, it seems to draw me up,
draw me up into the heavens.

So deep this brilliant blue sky,
through which light, sunlight
falls into my gravity well, falls
on trees radiating colors.

Leaves glowing from within
with the power of the sun,
with sunlight 93 million miles
from home making neon leaves.

Glancing off tombstones,
bringing energy to heat sink
gravestones, soaking warmth
for those without warmth below.

So inviting this field of stones,
final resting place of the dead,
its unusual charm enticing,
its headstones calling my name.

The Abandoned House

A quill blunted by a lifetime of writing,
now frozen at the bottom of a dry inkwell,
long forgotten by author and readers alike,
notices not the rising and setting of the sun.

Undisturbed dust stratifies the tabletop,
crisscrossed by naught but insect tracks
and grooves of breezes present and past,
a sheet of paper outlined, invisible below.

A wax sculpted candle holder, tallowed
by generations of candle sticks, lighting
the poets labor night after night, from
dusk till dawn, inspiring flame now dark.

Single hinged shutters banging in the wind,
the moon Morse Coding its lonely message,
keeping time with the passage of decades,
soon to fall silent to the ground below.

Broken and cracked window panes, doorways
for bats, rats and cats among other things,
welcomes rain and shine, moon and sun
into the small attic room, a writer's room.

Its writer long gone, a life force spent,
walled with books of others as well as own,
a sanctuary unknown, even to the bums
that sleep in the abandoned house below.

A ghost floats silently along the centuries,
hollow eyes taking in Time's slow passage,
long after the house leans to rubble,
it moans its lonely poems for you.

Carry Me Home

Tilly the bag lady stares from
the street corner of her life,
a male hustler side glances
then lowers his gaze.

Craning neck strangers
flow by like a river,
stick twirling beat cops
give a once over, twice.

Tour bus foreigners point
taking a picture to show later,
security cameras swivel,
whirring softly as I go by.

A blind man is taken aback
as I pass, dead eyes following,
seeing eye dog peeking,
hunkered under its forearm.

Jazz players wail my song,
black horses clop clop along,
spoke wheels creak and groan,
drawn hearse carries me home.

The Gates of Hell

A crusted plain stretches
as far as the eye can see,
glowing dark-red embers
of the Fires of Damnation.

Souls wander in the dusky glow,
milling about singly, in twos,
in threes, in small groups,
not a Demon to be seen.

After the briefest of lifetimes, and
fulfilling the prophecies of many,
I arrive at the Gates of Hell.
I don't know what I was expecting.

Where is the Fire and Brimstone?
Where are the tormented Souls?
Where is Satan? What gives here?
Not even an Underling to greet me!

I stand in a circle of stone altars
with four opposing breaks,
their well-worn paths
winding into the distance.

I see a flare up, way out
flames start twisting,
contorting into darkness,
eliciting a low moaning.

Flickering light reveals Lost Souls
like maggots on a carcass, squirming,
crawling into the flames, wailing
their passion of surrender and abandon.

The ground under my feet trembles.
Within the mound of burning Souls
a Demon tears them asunder, slinging
them into the void like fireballs.

I stand transfixed
realizing it is Satan!
I am shocked.
He looks so old, so tired.

He slaves on for an eternity,
filling the darkness, slinging
the Damned into
a great meteor shower.

Flames extinguish with an unearthly quiet
broken only by Satan's uncontrollable sobbing.
He retreats beneath the crust, whimpering.
It has been eerily quiet these last few Eons.

Death Brings An Angel

Why do I suffer so?
Death smiles sadly,
he speaks softly,
why, God wills it.

What have I done
to deserve such pain?
Remember, says the
Angel, remember.

All the lies, thefts,
betrayals, yes I see
memories flood you,
God remembers too.

My body betrays me,
burns clear to my soul,
like Eternal Damnation,
I pray Death takes me.

Will you take me Death?
Take me soon to Hell?
No, the Angel purrs,
I have come for you,

To take you to Heaven.
I bear God's gift for you,
He wants you close,
He is a vengeful God.

With My Passing

It seems so Buddhist, this desire
for the turning of the great wheel.

I sing songs of love long pent,
a thousand sorrowful songs of life.
Listen carefully to the whispering,
to the undertone of past and present.

Why am I not sorrowful
with my sweet embrace of Death?

Tick Tock Goes the Clock

Tick Tock, Tick Tock, Tick Tock,
Goes the Clock, Goes the Clock, Goes the Clock,
Tick Tock, Tick Tock
Goes the Clock, Goes the Clock.

Waiting, Waiting,
We all are Waiting,
Waiting, Waiting,
We all are Waiting.

Some all Day,
Some all Night,
Some all Night,
Some all Day.

Waiting, Waiting,
We all are Waiting,
Waiting, Waiting,
We all are Waiting.

Tick Tock, Tick Tock, Tick Tock,
Goes the Clock, Goes the Clock, Goes the Clock,
Tick Tock, Tick Tock
Goes the Clock, Goes the Clock.

Paul R. Hughes, Jr.
9/14/52 - 9/11/01

My brother worked on the 97th floor of the World Trade Center for Marsh McLennan Insurance Brokers as a manager in the computer system center.

He is one of the 400 out of 1700 missing from that company alone.

He leaves behind a wife and 10 yr. Old daughter.

As I travel to New York for a memorial service, this weekend, I want to thank you all for your thoughts, prayers and concerns.

My brother was honest, hard-working and impatient. He was a loving father, and faithful husband.

I remember the day he was born. I was at the end of our street with two friends, sitting on my bicycle, and I howled with delight that I had a brother. He was the cutest baby, and we all loved him a lot.

We had our childhood and future altered forever, when my dad chose to end his life. I was 16, Lynn was 13 and Paul was 6. I was unable psychologically to be the mentor that I later became, but eventually, we established a genuine, deep and loving relationship.

We laughed, joked and occasionally gave each other hell. Often, I counseled him, and other times he counseled me. His wisdom was always clear and often harsh but I never doubted he loved me. I often felt I needed a good shaking from my bigger, baby brother.

I can never remember having cross words that caused us anger. We knew we were going to be brothers, and good brothers for our entire lives.

I want to apprehend and punish those responsible.

Sincerely,
Don Hughes

My Brother

by Don Hughes and Albert de Lorenzo

I howled with delight the day he was born!
He was the cutest baby.
We were good brothers our entire lives.
I remember.

Dad chose to end his life when Paul was six.
Our future altered forever.
I was unable to mentor our Childhood's end.
His wisdom was always clear and often harsh.

I never doubted he loved me.
We knew.

My Own Daily View

by Don Hughes and Albert de Lorenzo

At the end of our street,
sitting on my bicycle,
I needed a good shaking.
We all loved him a lot.

Before we retaliate,
hold up the mirror.
See any character and integrity,
have we sold our soul?

Impatient

by Don Hughes and Albert de Lorenzo

I had a brother.
Honest and hard working.
We laughed and joked,
gave each other hell.

A deep and loving relationship,
I counseled him, he counseled me.
I do not remember any cross words
that caused us anger.

I want to know.
Why?

Young and Restless

by Don Hughes and Albert de Lorenzo

While God 1 and God 2 were wrestling,
Donna ran off with the UPS man.
Our intelligence must have shown something,
yet we failed to deal with it.

He liked to watch soaps
while napping.
I loved to call when they were on.
He offered me Forgiveness.

In my sanctuary of respite and contemplation,
I remember
Impromptu matches to get along.
I wonder what may have stalled?

Ramesh

by Don Hughes and Albert de Lorenzo

Should we be temporally driven?
I won't go along Polly Anna.
It's frivolous and trivial to care of such things.
Baseball and money are no excuse to annex oil fields.

God was busy golfing and asked
what had I found, in my truck.
The love of money, the root of evil,
how to be thankful for the thorns?

Failure Rates

By Don Hughes and Albert de Lorenzo

Do you work as unto the Lord
by making multi-million $ bonuses?
Making millions by slashing jobs
by being pricks?

How much money, how many possessions are enough?
We shop at Wal-Mart, we buy from China,
our neighbor's businesses die and we go to church.
"Vengeance is Mine," saith the Lord.

Some Introspection

by Don Hughes and Albert de Lorenzo

I want to apprehend and punish those responsible.

He was a loving father, a faithful husband, my bigger
baby brother.

I want to rid the world of these bastards,

in a way that is pleasing to God.

9780976225829